Contents

Introduction

When I visit schools to talk about the books I have written, one of the questions students often ask is, "Which was your first book?" "Well," I say, "the first book I ever wrote was called *Who Am I?* But you probably won't ever see it. I wrote it years ago because the Presbyterian Church asked me to write a book for young people about the Christian faith."

I answered this question so many times that finally I went back and reread that first book, and was reminded all over again of what the love of God has meant in the story of my own life.

My life is quite different from when I wrote that first book. When I began it, my husband and I had one tiny baby. By the time it was published, we had three little children. Today we have four children, all grown. Three of them are married, and our daughter Lin has a daughter of her own who is almost the age Lin was when she first came to our family from Hong Kong.

It was *Who Am I?* that started my life as a writer. After I had finished it, I realized that I loved to write and that writing, which was something I could do at home, suited my situation: with three, then four small children, I was not going back to teaching school anytime soon. Over a seven-year period I wrote many things that have never been published; then, at last, in 1973, my first novel appeared. I now have eighteen books with my name on the cover. These are books that I care about and am very grateful to have been able to write. Ten of them are novels for children and young people. I love to write novels because they allow me to explore and share some of my deepest feelings with my readers. In these stories I have had a chance to ask some of life's hard questions: Why do people suffer and die? What happens when you let jealousy rule your life? Can love really change a person? Does my life matter?

As I said, *Who Am I?* was my first book. Although it wasn't a novel, I was trying to ask some of the same questions in it that I ask in my novels. I love to re-write, and when I was given a chance to re-write *Who Am I?* I jumped at it. For no matter how much my life has changed since I first wrote this book, the one thing that hasn't changed during these ever-changing years is the love and leading of God.

What you have in your hands right now is both my first book and my latest book. Unlike *Bridge to Terabithia* and *Lyddie*, this book is not a novel, although, because I am primarily a storyteller, I cannot seem to talk long without including a bit of a story. If there is a central character in this book, it's me. The questions I ask here are ones that I have spent my life exploring. This new book is my invitation to you to join me in this exploration.

Where in the World Is God?

There was once a boy who, like many three-year-olds, was always asking questions. One day when he was eating his lunch he asked, "Mom, where's God?"

"God is everywhere," his mother said.

The boy thought a minute. "Is God in this house?"

"Yes."

"Is God in this kitchen?"

"Yes," his mother answered. "I told you, God is everywhere."

"Is God in my peanut-butter sandwich?"

"Well, yes, I suppose so. Didn't I just say that God is everywhere?"

"You'd better move over, God," the boy said. "I'm getting ready to bite."

We may laugh at a three-year-old's understanding, but not at his question. Where is God? Was God in the flood that washed away people's homes and ruined their stores and places of business? Was God in the fire that burned two children to death while their mother was away from the house? Was God in the bomb that dropped on the air-raid shelter, killing innocent people and maiming others? Where is God when a drunken driver plows into a school bus? Where is God when my mother, who has loved and served God all her life, is suffering and dying from cancer?

"How can you look at all the pain and suffering in the world and still say there is a God?" one of my friends asked me. "If there is a God, an all-powerful God, as you say, then that God is a monster!"

My friend is not alone. Looking at the world we know, many people decide that there is no God, certainly that there is no good God. A good God, they argue, would not permit all the evil and suffering in the world.

Many of us who call ourselves Christians are caught between the belief, on the one hand, that "this is my Father's world," and the knowledge, on the other hand, that there are many things about this world which seem to contradict our belief. There are times when we feel God's presence and goodness, but there are other times when even we who are Christians find ourselves asking, Where in the world is God?

Evidence of Evil in God's World

Christians believe that God is love, but the world we know is starving for lack of love. Think of the homeless, the hungry, the children who are neglected or abused. Even those people who claim to be God's children often bicker and backbite, ignore and despise one another. There are places even today where Christians blow each other up and claim to be doing "the will of God."

Christians believe that God is the God of truth, but the world we know seems far more interested in selling goods than in telling the truth. We listen to the leaders of our nation and shrug; "All politicians are liars," we say. A father told me about his four-year-old son who had been watching television. Suddenly the child got up, shut off the set, and exclaimed, "Brag, brag, brag — that's all they ever do." He marched off in disgust, having learned very young that you cannot believe much of what you hear.

Christians believe that God is the God of creation, but when we take a close look at nature, it seems unpredictable and often cruel. For those of us who have learned from babyhood that God is our "loving heavenly Father" who cares for even the smallest sparrow, natural disasters are hard to explain. If God created nature, can't God keep these occurrences in nature from hurting living creatures?

Surely there are times when we find ourselves asking the question "How could God let this happen?" I remember very well asking it myself.

I was a college student, working one summer in a small church in England and living with the pastor's family. One sunny afternoon there was a telephone call for the pastor. His face went gray as he listened to the caller's news. Two sixth-grade girls in the youth group had been playing together in the meadow beside the housing development. Alison had dared Pamela to climb to the top of the enormous tree that stood in the meadow. As Pamela neared the top, a branch gave way and she fell. The call was from the hospital. She had just died of a broken neck.

Pamela was dead, and Alison would have to live with the memory of her friend's death.

"If anyone dares tell me this is God's will, I'll tell him he's speaking blasphemy!" the pastor said. Now he said this in great distress from his own broken heart. He loved both those children. But I believe he was right. Pamela's death was not God's will, even though I saw God work in the midst of that tragedy.

Through the ministry of the church to Pamela's family, her parents came, for the first time, to have some understanding of the love of God. And the pastor and the congregation stood by Alison and comforted her in that lonely and frightening time, sharing with her their confidence that God could and did forgive her for her foolish dare.

Pamela's funeral was an amazing experience. All the children of the church were there. The organ played "The Lord's My Shepherd, I'll Not Want." At first only Pamela's young friends seemed able to sing, but gradually their voices gave the rest of us courage, and we joined in the hymn. By the time we got to the stanza "Yea, though I walk in death's dark vale, yet will I fear no ill," Pamela's parents were singing, too. We knew God was with us.

God did bring good out of this tragedy. But, like the pastor, I would not ever say that God "willed" it to happen. That is, I cannot believe that God wanted Pamela to die in this terrible way, or that God wanted Alison to have to suffer so much over her friend's death.

When our son David was eight years old, his best friend was a bright, funny little girl named Lisa Hill. While on vacation at the beach with her family, Lisa was struck and killed by lightning. My son could not understand why God would kill his friend. I truly did not believe that God had used that lightning bolt to kill Lisa, but why did she have to die? And why in such a terrible way? That's why I wrote *Bridge to Terabithia*. I was trying to find meaning in a tragedy that seemed to have no answer. I tried to say to my son, "God is not a monster. God does not go around striking little girls dead." But eight-year-old David decided that God was punishing him by killing his friend.

"No," I said. "God is not like that!"

But how do I know what God is like?

The only way I know is by looking at Jesus. When I read the gospel story, I see that Jesus spent a great deal of time healing the sick. Luke tells us that Jesus once broke up a funeral procession and restored the dead man to life. When he met men and women whose lives had been torn apart by their own wrongdoing, he forgave them. Jesus treated sin and suffering and death as enemies to be overcome.

God Has Created an Orderly Universe

Yet as we look at the world today, sin and suffering and death are everywhere present. If indeed they are enemies of God, why doesn't God defeat them once and for all? Is God powerless against the forces of nature and the evil of human beings? Does God stand by sadly but helplessly and watch the senseless suffering of innocent people?

You have probably heard or asked these same questions. They are the kinds of questions that sensitive and intelligent people will ask when they have struggled with what seems to be a problem with no solution. I can't pretend to know the answer to the problem of evil and suffering, but it may help to look more closely at the question itself.

The God of power and love created this universe and placed in the fabric of creation certain patterns of order. These patterns are absolutely necessary for life as we know it. When we ask, "Why couldn't God have kept this from happening?" we may actually be asking why God does not destroy this order and, in doing so, destroy us.

For instance, have you ever tried to play a game with someone who kept changing the rules? When I was young there was one boy on our block who always felt he could run the street football game to suit himself. He would make up a rule, then change it ten minutes later when it got in his way. How did he get away with revising the rules to suit himself? He owned the football. The rest of us were helpless, because if we complained, he would take his ball and go home. Any resemblance between proper football and what we ended up playing was purely coincidental.

"To be sure of winning," someone has said, "invent your own game and never let anyone else know the rules." God's power could do that; God's love will not.

Now there is a certain order in the universe. We could say that God made rules for the operation of the universe and built these rules in from the beginning. Suppose we could not count on God to keep these rules? There would be nothing in the world that we could depend on. Because we *can* count on the force of gravity, we can plan our lives with the confidence that it will be the same every day. In fact, we never have to give gravity a thought unless we happen to have an astronaut in orbit. But when a girl falls from a high tree, the force of gravity does not suddenly change to save her.

But what about miracles? someone might ask. Jesus went around healing people. He even raised people from the dead. The Gospels tell of his turning water into wine at a wedding feast and feeding five thousand people from a boy's picnic lunch.

And yet, there were certainly people in Palestine that Jesus did not heal, hungry people he did not feed, those he did not work miracles for. One of the thieves crucified with Jesus said to him, "Are you not the Christ? Save yourself and us." But Jesus did not come down from the cross or save those crucified with him. After his death, Jesus' followers performed many miracles, as the book of Acts relates, and yet most of them died as martyrs or as prisoners in jail. The apostle Paul says he prayed repeatedly that God would take away a "thorn in his flesh," some illness or difficulty that he longed to be rid of. But God chose not to relieve his suffering.

Through the centuries, people have prayed. Sometimes they feel that God has answered their prayers for healing or help. But other times people pray and no miracles occur. It is then that people are tempted to lose faith.

Why should God want me (or someone else) to suffer? If God is loving and God is powerful, why is there so much pain and evil in the world? I'm not sure that's a question which can be answered. As one theologian has said, "The fundamental miracle is Jesus himself." God choosing to become one of us in self-giving, forgiving love. So that when terrible things happen, even when I can't understand why, it is a comfort to me to remember that God in Jesus chose and, I believe, still chooses to be with those who suffer.

God's Gifts — Freedom and Responsibility

In Bunraku, the Japanese puppet theater, the puppets are nearly life-sized. A master puppeteer and his assistants manipulate the limbs and features of each puppet with such skill that the audience becomes absorbed in the story which is being acted out. The actors and actresses portray their parts perfectly, obeying every motion of the puppeteer's hands. They have no other choice, because they are made of wood and are absolutely under the puppeteer's control.

If God had made people like puppets, we could have been made absolutely obedient to God's will. But God did not want puppets; God wanted sons and daughters who would love and serve God freely and gladly. Unlike a puppeteer, God does not force people to play out a part already determined for them. People are free to love and obey, but there is also the very real chance that they will choose not to love or obey God. People are free to love and help one another. But there is also the chance that they will hate and hurt each other.

We may ask, "Couldn't God have made people want to love the Creator and all the creation? Couldn't God have kept them from hating?" The answer is "no," not if God truly made human beings with the ability to make choices. God has chosen to put us in a world where sin and suffering can and do exist, but it is also a world bursting with good things that can enrich our minds and hearts.

We are told in Genesis that the first command to the man and woman God had created was "Be fruitful and multiply, and fill the earth and subdue it; and have dominion over the fish of the sea and over the birds of the air and over every living thing that moves upon the earth" (Gen. 1:28). Some people think that this command gives human beings permission to exploit nature for their own ends. But I think it means that God intends for us to be agents of creation, to work with and for the creation to accomplish certain things. We were not put into a world where everything has already been done for us. On the contrary, we are meant to be partners with the Creator. Whenever scientists seek to unlock the mysteries of nature, whenever people sail the oceans and soar through space, whenever they write books or music or create art, whenever men and women work to improve human life and open up the secrets of the universe for the good of living creatures, they are, at least to some measure, obeying God's command.

When we were made partners of the Creator on this planet, God entrusted us with a great task. But we know in our lives and we can quickly see in the world about us today how foolish and weak and even evil people can be. Instead of harnessing the forces of nature for the good of all life, we have snatched nature's secrets and used them for destructive or selfish ends.

Where God Is in the World

What is God doing while people are making a mess of creation? I think if I were God, I would probably do one of two things. Either I would wash my hands of the whole affair and let people suffer the full consequences of their stupidity and stubbornness, or else I would take over completely. After all, if people can't live up to the responsibility that has been given to them, why should they be free? Let them be like rabbits. Rabbits have instincts, but they don't have the freedom to choose good or evil.

Fortunately, I am not God. God's solution is quite different from either of mine. God has neither deserted us nor taken away our freedom and responsibility. Instead, God has chosen to complete the work of creation through us.

In the Bible we are told that God called Abraham to be the father of the Hebrew nation. "I will bless you, and make your name great," God promised Abraham, *"so that you will be a blessing"* (Gen. 12:2, my emphasis). Through the history of the Hebrew people, God worked out a marvelous plan to bless all the peoples of the earth. During their time of captivity in Babylon more than a thousand years after Abraham, some of the Jews realized that God had chosen them not for special favors but for a special mission. One of the prophets gave them this word from God:

> "It is too light a thing that you should be my servant
> to raise up the tribes of Jacob
> and to restore the preserved of Israel;
> I will give you as a light to the nations,
> that my salvation may reach to the end of the earth."
> (Isa. 49:6)

We believe that God called the Jewish people to be in a unique way the representatives of God's plan in the world. By God's covenant with them, they were made a special people to carry out God's work. Not all of the Hebrew people remained faithful to the covenant. But even in the darkest periods of their history, there were always a few — a remnant, the Bible says — who remembered who they were: the people of the Lord God. They believed that the Lord God was the maker of heaven and earth, the savior of the Hebrew people, and that someday all the world would know him.

They believed that their God was at work in human history. They expected their Lord to work in the events of their lives. Hadn't God miraculously saved their ancestors from slavery in Egypt? Hadn't he given them a time of glory through the reign of King David? Hadn't God judged their unfaithfulness by permitting them to fall to their enemies? Hadn't God disciplined them during their exile and then delivered them from Babylonian bondage and helped them rebuild their nation? Therefore, as they suffered under the tyranny of Rome, the Jewish people remembered their history. They prayed for release and waited for God to deliver them once again.

Even though many of the Jews were eagerly waiting for God to act, God caught them by surprise. The Creator of heaven and earth acted in a way that they could not have imagined. The Lord God entered their history — as a baby boy.

Now we have heard so often that Jesus was God Incarnate (literally God in the flesh) that it fails to shock us, but it should. It certainly shocks our Jewish and Muslim neighbors to hear us talk about the one true God walking around on earth in human form. Do we Christians realize what we are saying? God, the Maker of all things, the Ruler and Judge of history, became a part of this creation, a part of human history. In a tiny Palestinian village a baby was born, the son of a peasant woman, and this baby, we say, was God come into the world to live and, yes, to die as a man.

The world into which Jesus of Nazareth was born was, for most of the Jews, a world of injustice and poverty. Rome had imposed peace on her conquered nations, but this peace was punctured from time to time by uprisings of oppressed peoples. Jesus was one of the oppressed. He knew how it felt to be hungry and tired and homeless. His friends often misunderstood him. When his death was near, most of them deserted him. The religious and political leaders of his day regarded him as a dangerous heretic. He was tried by prejudiced courts and sentenced to death.

For Christians, the story of Jesus of Nazareth is the pivotal point in the plan of God for this world. As one early writer put it,

> In many and various ways God spoke of old to our fathers
> by the prophets; but in these last days he has spoken to us
> by a Son, whom he appointed the heir of all things,
> through whom also he created the world. (Heb. 1:1-2)

Throughout human history, then, God has been speaking to persons words of love and judgment. But the birth of Jesus of Nazareth is a new Word. Here God speaks directly to humankind by being born as a baby, growing up, and living and dying as one of us. The death of Jesus was not simply the cruel act of political and religious officials of his day. The Bible tells us plainly that the death of Jesus is God's answer to all the sin and evil of the world: "He is himself the remedy for the defilement of our sins, not our sins only but the sins of all the world" (1 John 2:2, NEB).

God's answer to sin and evil does not end with the death of Jesus. If it did, evil and sin would prove more powerful than God, and they are not. God's love is more powerful than the worst sin that humanity can devise. It is even more powerful than the forces of nature. One ancient hymn-writer says so in these words:

> The powers of death have done their worst,
> But Christ their legions hath dispersed:
> Let shouts of holy joy outburst,
> Alleluia!
>   (stanza 2, "The Strife Is O'er, the Battle Done")

"The powers of death," both human sin and death itself, did all they could against Jesus Christ. But he defeated them by rising from the dead, offering forgiveness and new life to all people, even those who had betrayed him or killed him.

The world in which we find ourselves is a world in which sin and evil and death still exist. Living in the midst of daily disappointments and scary headlines, it is easy to focus on the things that are wrong and forget that this is the world which God loves. It was into this same imperfect world that Jesus was born, and it was for the sake of this world that he died. It is this world that will be under Christ's rule when God's purpose for humankind and for the whole of creation is completed.

Who Are We?

But it is possible to talk in big, general terms about the "world" and still not know what all this has to do with us, you and me. When you get your copy of the class picture, whose face do you look for first? Once you finally locate yourself, doesn't the whole picture suddenly become more interesting? In a similar but far more important way, the vast mural of God's action in nature and in the history of the world comes alive when each of us finds himself or herself in the picture.

In his great musical work entitled *St. Matthew's Passion,* Bach tells the story of Jesus' suffering and death. Sometimes the chorus represents the disciples; at other times it sings the

cruel taunts of the soldiers or the angry cries of the mob; at
still other times the chorus represents believers of that time
or a later time looking back on the crucifixion with sorrowful
wonder. In his music, Bach is saying, "We are there." We are
not there simply as onlookers. We are, rather, taking many
parts in the action. Sometimes we are fearful disciples. At
other times we join the heartless executioners or the igno-
rant, angry mob. At still other times we are believers, filled
with love and praise for God. Each of us has within his or her
heart the varied music of doubt and faith, fear and trust, hate
and love. Each of us finds himself or herself part of the sin
and evil that reject God's love and help to crucify Christ. But
each of us is a member of the human family that God has
placed in the world to be God's partners — to care for this
creation and to work for the good of all God's creatures.

What about Me?

In the hospital delivery room, the excitement mounted. Suddenly a shout went up: "It's a boy!" Answering the shout of the nurses, there came an angry, determined little cry. Dr. Johnson held up a tiny pink baby. We had waited so long for him and here he was at last — our baby.

Yet by the time he was just five minutes old, he was not simply "our baby" but "John": six pounds of unmistakably male body, equipped with lungs and heart and liver. His talents and intelligence and certain strengths and weaknesses that he would carry to his grave were already wrapped in this small package. He was unique. God had created a new human life.

Statistically, the birth of a baby is a very ordinary event. It happens many times every day in every country of the world. But — and here is the marvel — each baby is a completely new event. Each baby — that means each of us — is a special act of God. Each is separate from every other person. Which means that each of us will have to answer for herself or himself the question "Who am I?"

Created by God

You may have noticed my heavy hints in Chapter One that in order to answer the question "Who am I?" we have to have some knowledge of the One who made us. The Bible tells us that we are created by God, the Creator of all things. Scientists are just beginning to understand some of the ways in which God brought the world into existence. The more they tell us, the more we must marvel at the power and wisdom of God, who not only brought all things into being but who continues to maintain the orderly working of the universe.

The Bible also tells us that God loves the creation, watching over it and caring for it. And the Bible says that of all creation, nothing is more precious to God than humankind. People alone can freely love and praise God. We are created, the Bible tells us, in the very image, the likeness of God. When I say that God loves humankind, I don't mean that God loves a big, unspecified lump. God knows us each by name. "Why," says Jesus, "even the hairs of your head are all numbered" (Matt. 10:30). I can see Jesus saying this with a twinkle in his eye. I don't care how many hairs I have on my head, but it is wonderful to me to realize that God knows me inside and out and that I am very dear to the Creator of the universe.

Now take a look at yourself. God created you. God loves you. God is keeping you alive and causing you to grow and develop. You are God's beloved child.

Created to Be and to Belong

If you are like most people, you want to get to know yourself, and undoubtedly you have already asked the question "Who am I?" in some form or other. A baby begins to ask it when she discovers the parts of her own body. A two-year-old often says "No" to everything. He is making an attempt to be somebody — to be a *me* even when he has to declare war on all the big *you's* of the world to win the right to be a *me*. This is a very personal struggle. We may laugh when we watch a toddler shaking her head and stamping her foot, but she is in fact engaged in a struggle that every human being must undertake. The struggle is necessary because each of us was created by God to *become* a person. As persons, we are more than human animals. As persons, we are creatures who can direct and determine to some extent what we will do and what we will become.

Perhaps you can understand better what it means to be a

person if you compare a human being with other forms of animal life. With very little effort, animals become what God created them to be. A kitten does not have to struggle to become a kitten. It will do most things by instinct. All it has to do to become a cat is to grow physically. A human being, however, will not become a person on instinct alone. If a baby were to grow up "naturally," it would act very much like an animal. We know this from the few examples we have of children who have grown up without human contact.

Each baby is given the potential to become a person. In the company of other people, a child can learn how to direct his or her own life and how to live with others. If this process breaks down, either because the child lacks loving adult care or because of some failure in the child to begin to take responsibility for his or her actions, the adult individual will be less than the person God intended.

There is a part of our life that is set and fixed. For example, people have no wings. But because we have freedom and can think, explore, and invent, we *can* fly. In a similar way, every human being is born with certain features. You have inherited from your biological parents a unique combination of body and mind which is you. Your bone structure and the color of your eyes, hair, and skin are part of your genetic heritage. Your talents and your mental ability are part of who you are. There are many things about yourself that you had no choice in and that you cannot change, but remember that it is you whom God created. God has a purpose for exactly the combination of body, mind, and spirit that is you. God can help you know how best to use the body and mind you have been given. God can help you grow as a person who directs his or her own life and yet lives in a relationship of love and trust with other persons.

None of us can become a person alone. We are always living in company with other people. We cannot understand the meaning of our own lives unless we look at the persons and events that have helped to mold our lives. God has placed each of us in a particular family, in a certain community, in this particular time in history. None of us chose our own parents, the communities we were born into, or our native lands. Yet all of these influence our lives. They will have a powerful effect on our thinking, our speech, our actions.

But we can also influence them. We can change our families by the love or hate we bring into them. We can change our society by the way we act in it.

At this point in your life, you are probably very aware of being either a boy or a girl. Your closest friends are likely to be of your own sex. As your body develops, your interest in the opposite sex tends to develop as well. You'll soon be one of those peculiar creatures — teenagers — who seem to be thinking about bodies (their own or someone else's) most of the time.

Adolescence is a special time in our society. In some cultures there is no such thing. One day a person is a child; the next day he or she is considered an adult. In our society, teenagers may have adult bodies, but for the most part they are not expected to have either the freedom or the responsibilities of adulthood.

Someone has said that all the really important choices in life have to be made when you're too young to make them. You are on the threshold of that time of choices. Many young people make bad choices because they don't know who they are. They don't know that they are God's beloved children, so they do not value themselves as they should. They allow themselves to be used by others. They abuse their own bodies, the irreplaceable gift God has given them.

God invented sex by creating humankind male and female. The fact that both men and women are needed to make society complete helps us to know that no one human being can become a real person alone. You were created through the union of two persons. You were created for companionship with other persons. You cannot change the fact that you need friends, family, and community. You can choose to act as if other people don't mean much to you. You can treat people like things that you can push around. You can use people to get what you want. But unless you learn to accept love from others and to extend love to them in return, you will never become the person God created you to be.

Created for God

Do you remember the story of the Ugly Duckling? The poor creature was too large, his neck was too long, and he was awkward and clumsy. He became the target of all the jokes in the duck community. Then one day he learned a secret. The reason he was such a failure as a duck was that he was never intended to be one. He was not a duck at all, but a swan. Once he learned his true identity, life was completely different. The other swans in the castle moat greeted him with joy and respect. How happy he was to know who he was and where he belonged!

The story of humankind is something like the story of the Ugly Duckling. People, male and female, were created in the "image of God." That is, we were created to live in fellowship with God and to be a part of God's family. But all through human history people have failed to live as God's children. Many have tried to act as if they neither belonged to God nor needed God in any way. Others, like the unfortunate duckling, simply have not discovered that they were created for a particular kind of life. Yet God has created each one of us to be children in a family, and we will never be complete or real persons until we take our proper places in the household of God.

As Christians we believe that we can know God through the Bible, which tells the story of God's work in the world on our behalf; through the church, which is the family of God at work in partnership with the Creator; and through the Holy Spirit, which is God's own spirit at work in our world and in our hearts.

The opportunities to know God are open for you, but no one can force you to take advantage of them. God has made you who you are. God has given you freedom to decide how you will use the gifts to love and reason, to explore and create, to choose and change. God wants you to use your gifts to become a responsible, joyful person who will love God and love and serve others. But God respects you and allows you to make the choice.

Life does not give us just one choice, however. Every day there are many times when we must choose. And there are times when all of us choose to turn away from God and to use the freedom that God has given us for selfish ends. There are times when we pretend that we have no need of God, that we can do everything ourselves. We often hurt other people; we even hurt ourselves. We cannot dodge the fact that part of the answer to the question "Who am I?" is a pretty sad one. In the language of the Bible, we are sinners who over and over again need God's forgiveness and help in making a new start.

On Becoming You

Whether you are a boy or a girl, tall or short, fat or thin, brilliant or average, good-looking or plain, the important thing is that you are you. You have inherited certain characteristics, and the home or homes you grow up in will have a large part in shaping you. There are things about yourself that you like and some that you don't like. There are some things you can change (and perhaps ought to) and other things you can't help. But it is *you* (not some dream of what you wish you were) that God made and loves. It is you that Jesus Christ calls to be his friend and follower. It is you that God wants to become fully yourself — the person you were created to be.

We have an adopted daughter named Lin. When she first came to us from Hong Kong, she was so frightened that she couldn't sleep. Twice before in her two years of life, everything she had known had suddenly disappeared. As an infant, she had lost her first home and family. Now the familiar sights and sounds of the children's home were gone. How could she dare close her eyes? Everything might suddenly disappear again.

We tried to convince her that she was now our little girl. We put a long mirror in the play area. She would look in the mirror as if to make sure she was herself and that she was right here. Before she would speak to any of us, she began whispering to herself in the mirror.

Gradually she began to relax. She started making faces at herself. She even took a tiny rubber dog and talked to him as she stood before the mirror. At last she began to run about the house happily as though she owned it. She was able to fall asleep without crying. Before much longer, she no longer needed the mirror to reassure her. She knew who she was and where she belonged. She was a member of the family that lived in this house.

We are God's children, and although there are many times when we don't act like beloved children, God wants us to know that we don't have to be afraid. We belong to God not because we have chosen God but because God has chosen us. Through the death of Jesus, God says, "This is how much I love you. This is what I am willing to do for you." And through the resurrection of Christ, God says, "There is nothing — not sin, death, or all the power of evil — that can defeat my love for you."

Now God wants you to grow up in this love, using the good gifts you have been given to live joyfully and give joy to others. If you are like Lin, asking yourself in the mirror "Who am I?" the answer is this: "Beloved, we are God's children now; it does not yet appear what we shall be, but we know that when he appears we shall be like him, for we shall see him as he is" (1 John 3:2).

Where Do I Belong?

Amy knew she was taking a chance asking Beth to come home with her today. But somehow she needed to try it. Beth was her best friend since her family had moved here. Then, as soon as Amy opened the door, Amanda appeared. She was taller than Amy, but she ran toward her in a clumsy, lumbering imitation of a four-year-old.

"Ameee! Ameee!" she cried. "See my new dress! See my new dress!"

Amy could feel Beth stiffen beside her. "This is Amanda," Amy said, her face burning, and then, "my sister."

"What's your name?" Amanda asked.

Beth couldn't seem to decide whether to look at Amanda or at the hall bookcase, but finally she turned toward the older girl. "Beth," she mumbled.

"Hi, Bef," Amanda said happily. "See my new dress?"

Watching Beth, Amy missed none of the unspoken messages she was sending out — fear, disgust, pity. What was the matter? Hadn't Beth ever seen someone with Down syndrome before? She had thought Beth would understand. But why? Oh, people pretended it was just fine to have a sister like Amanda. But they always acted weird when Amanda was around.

Amy loved Amanda. She had loved her ever since she could remember. Still, sometimes she wished that Mom and Dad would put Amanda in one of those schools. Not forever, but just for a while . . . just until Amy could get adjusted to her new neighborhood . . . just until she could figure out who her real friends were going to be.

*   *   *

It wasn't fair, Jason thought, that he had to be the one to decide. He loved both his parents. He had been only four when they separated. They'd made a big thing of saying, "We're divorced from each other — not from you." They'd made a big thing of sharing everything about him. Three-and-a-half days at the house with Mom, and three-and-a-half days at the apartment with Dad. He had lots of clothes and lots of toys, but he never knew where anything was.

He got used to it — sort of. He even got used to his stepmother and then his stepfather. When his little stepbrother hit him, he never hit him back. When his little stepsisters tore up his model cars, he didn't touch their junk — he just carted his models over to his tiny bedroom at the apartment. When his half brother was born and everyone said the baby looked "just like Jason," he tried to act pleased even though the kid looked just like a bald, red-faced dwarf to him.

But now his stepfather was being transferred to Texas. No more half a week in each place — that would be a relief. But he had to decide where to live during the school year. His parents had left the decision up to him, but each of them had hinted that if he chose to live with the other parent, it would be devastating.

*   *   *

"You can't do this to me!" Mike banged his glass on the table.

"Mi-ike — " His father broke his name into two syllables, raising his voice on the second syllable to issue a warning.

"Mike, for goodness' sake. You'll break something." His mother's voice was heavy with fatigue.

"You can have the big bureau," Matthew said, being the perfect little kid as usual and making Mike look awful.

"I don't want to room with Matthew. You can't make me."

"Mi-ike — " his father said again.

"You ought to put her in a nursing home or something. That's where she belongs. She doesn't even know us half the time."

"We can't afford — "

"State hospital, then. Mom, she acts crazy most of the time. You can't take care of her. You said so yourself. I heard you."

"She's your grandmother, Mike. She's your father's mother. We can't just — just — "

"Mike," his father interrupted, "this isn't going to be easy for any of us. Your mother least of all. But she's willing to try. It seems to me that for the sake of this family you could put up with a minor inconvenience. . . ."

Minor inconvenience! That's how his parents described his whole life being destroyed. He didn't care if it was his grandmother. She didn't act like the grandmother he remembered as a little kid. She was nuts. You would tell her the same thing over and over again and still she'd complain that no one ever told her anything. She dressed funny, and sometimes she forgot to bathe or comb her hair. He'd be embarrassed to bring friends over. His mother would have no time for Mike or his dad, or even for Matthew. Caring for Grandma would be more than a full-time job. And Mike would never ever have a minute of privacy. How could his parents do this to him?

*   *   *

"Is there something wrong, Sarah?" Mrs. Craig had asked Sarah to stay a few minutes after school, and now she was quizzing her. "I mean," she continued, "at home."

Sarah didn't answer. What was she supposed to say to a teacher about what was happening at home?

"I'd like to help, if I can," Mrs. Craig went on and then waited for Sarah to speak up.

Am I supposed to tell you my father lost his job? Sarah wondered to herself. That he's looked and looked for a new one and no one will hire him? He has a college degree, and they won't even hire him as a security guard. Am I supposed to tell you that what my mother makes as a receptionist is hardly enough to feed us, much less pay the mortgage? Do you want to know that our house won't sell and we may lose it to the bank any day now? Do you want me to say that my dad is drinking too much and that last night he hit my mother? And how is a teacher supposed to help? Nobody can.

"Sarah?"

"It's okay, Mrs. Craig. I'm just not feeling too good today. I'll be all right."

The Benefits of Belonging

A few years ago, a leading automobile manufacturer advertised its cars with the slogan "Ask the man who owns one." The manufacturer believed that anybody who owned that make of car would be happy and would brag about it to anyone who asked. People with strong, happy families, however, often take them for granted. Sometimes the person who doesn't "own one" can best tell you why it is important to belong to one.

Human beings, unlike many animals, need to belong to other people, and our families give us people to whom we belong and who belong to us. Where would we be without them?

The story is told that Frederick II, a thirteenth-century emperor, decided to conduct a scientific experiment. He wanted to know what language children would speak naturally if no one taught them a particular language. He collected a group of newborn orphans and hired nurses to care for them. The nurses were told to give the babies plenty of food, clean clothes, and warm beds, but the nurses were never to speak aloud in the nursery or to show any affection for the children.

The foolish emperor's experiment failed. He never learned the original language of humankind because all the babies died. We might say they starved for lack of genuine human contact. People have to belong to somebody.

It is the love of our parents that first introduces many of us to God's love. If we have parents who know and love God, it is easier for us to come to trust God's care for our lives. One summer a class I was teaching made the story of the Prodigal Son (Luke 15:11-32) into a play. After it had been performed and we came together to discuss it, one of the girls said, "The father in the play was just like my daddy." It wasn't hard for her to imagine God as a loving parent because she had had one all her life.

As children grow up within a loving family, they become persons partly by imitating their parents. They learn to smile because they are smiled at. They learn to speak by listening to their parents and brothers and sisters and imitating the sounds they hear. I know a boy whose first word was "amen." His family finally figured out why. At the end of the blessing — after the "amen" — the food was served. Ben thought that saying "amen" was the way you called for supper.

A little child also learns she is an individual, separate from her parents, when she dares to say "no" to them. She may not even mean "no," but it is important for her to say "no" to prove that she can. If you ask a two-year-old, "Do you want to eat your lunch now?" he may very well say, "No!" But if you put out your hand, he will take it quite cheerfully and trot over to his high chair.

A loving family gives us a place where we can safely try out our no's and yes's. Most parents put up with a lot from their children and do it gladly, because they want to see them grow up to be strong, independent men and women.

The Strains of Belonging

The very fact that in a family we do belong in a special way to one another makes for certain problems. Even in the best of families, and on the most ordinary days, there are strains and irritations. Dad may always be after you to clean your room, but his workspace in the garage is such a mess that you can't even find a screwdriver when you need it. Mom used to be a great cook, but ever since she started her new job, she never seems to have time to do more than mix up macaroni and cheese from a box. Your sister may borrow your new sweater before you've even worn it yourself, and your brother is quite likely to lose your favorite CD.

But these are minor irritations. As the stories at the beginning of this chapter hint, a lot of families (maybe yours) have real problems. A woman I know can't bring herself to recite the Lord's Prayer because the father she knew abused her when she was a child. Many children grow up in families where one or even both parents are alcoholic or on drugs. How can such children think of God as a loving parent?

A friend of mine was deserted by both her parents when she was a baby. The passages in the Bible that speak of God as father or that compare God to a loving mother seemed especially painful to her. Then one day she found this verse in Psalm 27, which seemed to speak directly to her: "Though my father and my mother forsake me," the Psalmist says, "the Lord will take me into his care" (v. 10, NEB).

When I think of persons who never had a loving family, I remember the little boy who was afraid to go to sleep in a room by himself. "Don't be afraid," his mother said. "Just remember that God is always with you."

The little boy began to cry. "But I want somebody with skin on," he said.

Surely one reason that God came in the flesh was because we human beings need someone "with skin on" to teach us about God's love. And God means for those of us who have been blessed with loving families and friends to be the ones "with skin on" for others who don't have loving families, so that we may teach them that God loves them, too.

*   *   *

No matter what your family is like, I'm sure you have already discovered that the members of your family aren't perfect. They are human beings with strong points and weaknesses, talents and limitations. Learning to love your parents and brothers and sisters as they are, not as you wish they were, is a part of growing up. We won't be able to love one another perfectly, of course; only God is capable of perfect love. But the good news of our faith is that God is able to love us — that God does love us — just as we are.

Even those who have heard from childhood of God's love often fail to trust that love. Sometimes we are afraid of God, like naughty children who are afraid of their parents' punishment. But God wants us to know that we are loved with all our faults and failings. God's care for us has nothing to do with our goodness or our worthiness. God loves us because we are God's beloved children. When we know this, it becomes possible for us to begin to love one another.

In our church we have a three-generation family named Caccavo. The youngest generation are Tony and Nicolas, who, when I first met them, were adorable preschoolers. Sometimes their parents were a little late to the Sunday service. From where I sat in the choir, I could see Nick and Tony struggling to get out of their winter jackets, pulling impatiently away from their mom and dad, and racing joyfully down the middle aisle to the pew where their grandfather was sitting, then climbing onto his lap.

I was watching this happy scene one Sunday morning when it occurred to me that that is what faith is. Tony and Nick know beyond a shadow of a doubt that their relationship with Ralph, their grandfather, has nothing to do with whether they've picked up their socks or eaten their oatmeal. Ralph sees them often, and he knows them very well — the good and the bad. Still they can't wait to be with him. He pulls them close to him, and all three of them glow with the pure delight of being together again.

The Caccavos would be a picture of what faith is in any case, but I happen to know that Ralph is Tony and Nick's grandfather not by heredity but by adoption.

In ancient Roman law, adoption was a solemn and serious business. Once it was accomplished, the status of the adopted child was exactly the same as that of a child born to the family, and of course the adopted child shared equally in any inheritance. In the book of Romans, Paul uses the image of adoption to say in still another way how God loves us and has made our relationship secure: "For you did not receive a spirit of slavery to fall back into fear," Paul says, "but you have received a spirit of adoption. When we cry, 'Abba! Father!' it is that very Spirit bearing witness with our spirit that we are children of God, and if children, then heirs, heirs of God and joint heirs with Christ" (8:15-17, NRSV). The word "Abba" is the Aramaic word for "Father," but it feels more like "Daddy." It's the name the boy Jesus probably called Joseph.

Respect for One Another

An anthropologist tells the story of visiting a tribe in Southeast Asia. She was invited to spend the night with one of the families. When she was taken to her room for the night, she was quite surprised to discover that although the room had three inside walls separating it from the rest of the house, there was no fourth wall. It was wide open to the outdoors.

"When you have walls inside the house, why don't you have an outside wall?" she asked her host. It was her host's turn to be surprised. "Why, who do you need protection from except those closest to you?" he asked.

We do sometimes need protection from those closest to us even when they are, for the most part, quite nice people. Ironically, the very fact that we are most at ease at home and don't have to impress our families sometimes makes us less kind to them than we would be to a total stranger.

An important part of kindness is respect. Each member of the family needs to respect each other member. Even the smallest child deserves respect. There was once a mother who seemed to have an unusually respectful relationship with her toddler. Someone asked her how she could be so patient with his demands and stubbornness. "I try to think of him as an ambassador from another country," she said. "He hasn't yet learned our language or our customs, so he can't express himself well, and he often behaves inappropriately. But still, in his own country he's an ambassador, so I have to treat him politely even when he seems impossible."

The Home Hard to Live In

There are no perfect homes, but as we all know, some are easier to live in than others. In the stories at the beginning of this chapter, Amy, Jason, Mike, and Sarah are facing problems similar to those some of you might be experiencing.

If you have a handicapped brother or sister, or one who has been ill for a long time, you probably understand Amy's mixed feelings toward her sister Amanda. She loves Amanda, but sometimes she can't help feeling embarrassed by her. And even if she were more mature and never embarrassed by her sister, still, she would always have to take second place in her parents' time and attention. A child who is handicapped or ill simply demands more of a parent's care than his brothers or sisters. Amy might understand this completely, but it would be strange if she never resented always having to take a backseat to her sister's needs.

Jason has a problem because he belongs to two homes. As he remembers his parents' bitter arguments (sometimes over him) and the divorce that followed, he may feel somehow at fault. Of course, it isn't Jason's fault that his parents' marriage failed, but after such a painful occurrence, children often ask themselves, "What did I do wrong?"

As people live longer, many of the problems of old age become a real problem in a family. The doctor probably has concluded that Mike's grandmother has Alzheimer's disease. Currently there is no known cure for this condition. Unless one is found, Mike's grandmother will continue to deteriorate mentally until she dies. To see someone they have loved turn into a stranger is a frightening experience for Mike's family, but they love Grandma, and they want to take care of her as well as they can. This will make an enormous difference in every family member's life. Who could blame Mike for objecting to what he knows will be a drastic change in his life and the lives of his whole family? And yet there is no easy solution. What can a family do when a grandparent needs their care?

Not so long ago, Sarah's family lived an ordinary, middle-class life. Then, suddenly, everything changed. The money which made that comfortable life possible just wasn't there anymore. Now everything, including her father's personality, seems threatened by negative change. She would like to help, but how? A hundred years ago she would have quit school and gotten a job as a factory worker or a housemaid. But things are much different today, and Sarah feels helpless.

Some of you reading this book may be able to know how Amy, Jason, Mike, or Sarah feels. Others may have even more difficult problems at home than any of these. You may not even have a home or a family to call your own. Does this book have anything to say to you? Let me try out two thoughts.

The first comes from an English writer named Hugh Redwood. Mr. Redwood tells about an occasion in his life when he was faced with many problems for which there seemed to be no answers. Once when he was visiting a friend, he found on a table in the guest room a Bible opened to Psalm 59. Verse 10 of that psalm reads, "My God in his steadfast love will meet me." Someone had written beside the verse these words: "My God in his loving-kindness will meet me at every corner." To Mr. Redwood this seemed to be a message from God. No matter how difficult his problems were, God would meet him at the corners he could not see around and help him make the turn.

The second comes from a childhood friend of mine. When we were young, I was unaware of something that she has since told me about — that back in those days her father was an alcoholic who abused her mother and terrified her and her brother. "But Beverly, you were always such a great person," I said. And she was. "How could you turn out the way you did with a family like that?"

"It was the church," she said. "I started going to Sunday school when I was very young, and the church became my family. I don't know what I would have done without them."

Like my friend, each of you belongs to another family — the family of God. Now this larger family is also an imperfect one. There will surely be occasions when people in the church will hurt you or disappoint you. But there will also be times when members of this family will be the bearers of God's loving-kindness to you, as they were for my friend Beverly. When God meets us at the corners of our lives, he nearly always does so through another person. Christians are called by God to share one another's burdens. When you cannot share some problem with your immediate family, look around you carefully. There may well be someone in the larger family who stands ready to help.

The very fact that you are reading this book says to me that you are looking for God's love in your life. I believe that God is eager for you to know this love for yourself. Exactly how this will happen, I don't know. Maybe the person from whom you got this book wants to share God's love with you. Perhaps you have a teacher or a friend at school who is already sharing God's love with you or is eager to do so if you will give him or her the chance.

Forbearing One Another

There are times of turmoil even in the best of homes. A poor report card, a bag of trash not taken out to the curb, an argument over which TV program to watch, a messy room — any number of minor crises can send a whole household into an uproar.

Living together in a family takes a lot of what the Bible calls "forbearance." This is really the willingness to put up with another person. Parents have the most practice in this virtue; babies take it for granted that parents will feed them promptly and change their diapers right away. If a baby wakes up hungry at two in the morning, does she say to herself, "Poor Mom and Dad, they need their sleep. I'll just stick it out until eight A.M."? No, she screams until one of her parents struggles out of bed and takes care of her needs. A baby knows nothing of patience or consideration for others.

In fact, a baby does not think about his parents as individuals with lives of their own. Parents are conveniences for him. Gradually, however, as children grow older, they realize that they are separate persons from their parents, and that brothers and sisters are individuals as well. Eventually, most children come to recognize that what they want can't always come first. Each member of a family has needs and wants; each member needs to learn the give and take of family life. We don't expect infants to realize this, but an individual who thinks "give and take" means "You give, I take" has never grown up, whatever his age.

There will be times when parents ask a child to do something she really doesn't want to do. For example, you might be asked to go on a family visit to your grandmother's when you'd already planned to go on a camping trip. You can't understand why you should have to give up your plans, and your parents are using words and phrases like "selfish" and "your grandmother's happiness." In this sort of situation, forbearance is needed. Neither side can fully understand the other, but for the sake of the family, they forbear. That is, they put up with the actions and ideas of the other person — which they do not like — for the sake of the person, whom they do like.

The word "forbearance" has a solemn-faced, old-fashioned feel about it, as though it flourishes in the lives of those who enjoy making martyrs of themselves. I had an elderly relative who would always say, "Oh, no, don't give me the breast of chicken; I really prefer the neck." It used to make my sisters and me roll our eyes and stifle a groan. Who was she kidding? Matthew, the perfect little brother who wants to show up Mike's selfishness, gives most of us a pain. Forbearance, like all the Christian virtues, grows best in the warmth of humor. If you can laugh at yourself or see the funny side of a family muddle, you can get through many of the strains of living in a family.

Martin Luther was the hero of the Reformation, but sometimes, when he felt weighed down by the burdens of life, he would slip into dark, despairing moods that infected his entire household. During one such period, he was startled out of his depression by the sight of his wife dressed in black.

"Why are you in mourning?" he asked. "Who has died?"

"God," Mrs. Luther replied.

"God?"

"Why, yes," she answered. "From the way you have taken over all the troubles of the world, I was sure God must have died."

Mrs. Luther lived with a man who was, as they say, a legend in his own time. Not only did she have to endure her husband's fame and his moods, but she also had to put up with the constant opposition of his enemies and the admiration of his friends. A number of these friends simply moved into the Luther household so they could be closer to their leader. But Mrs. Luther obviously managed to keep her sense of humor, and so she was able to keep the man who led the Reformation from taking himself too seriously. She gave her husband and children the gift of Christian forbearance clothed in laughter.

You and Your Home

You never get to choose the family you'll be born into or even, most probably, the family who adopts you. And yet, to a great extent, the family you grow up in sets the pattern for the person you will become.

This means there are certain things about ourselves that come to us through our families whether we want them or not. We may be grateful for some of the things that our families give us, while there are others that we might think we'd do anything to be rid of. Some families seem to have all the good luck and others nothing but bad. One family may be ruled by two very critical, domineering parents; another family may have a mother and father who are very supportive of and flexible with their children. One family may have three children, all of whom are happy and well adjusted; another family may have three children, all of whom are dissatisfied and rebellious despite the time and attention their parents have lavished on them. There seems to be no fairness when it comes to family. But this is part of the price of being human. We are not puppets who are affected only by the movements of the puppeteer. God has made us people in families whose lives affect one another's for good and for ill.

This doesn't mean, however, that people are nothing but what their families make them. The family sets a pattern, yes, but the pattern of family life is not a machine that holds each succeeding generation on an unchangeable track. The pattern is made up of living people. Each new child who comes into the family is an individual. The members of the family shape this child's life, but this child also helps to shape their lives. In addition, each member of a family is responsible for herself or himself. A young girl, for example, is what she is largely because of her family, but she must take the responsibility in her own life for what she does with what she has been given.

Some years ago, I taught a sixth-grade class that was kept lively by the antics of a boy named Fred. Fred had everything against him. His mother was dead, and his father had subsequently married a woman who hated Fred. And, to be truthful, Fred wasn't so loveable. He was blind in one eye and hard of hearing. He had failed the third grade twice, and since our school was small, he had had the same teacher all three years. She said, very frankly, that Fred was a terrible boy from an awful home. Fred wasn't all that fond of her, either.

One day I kept Fred after school. "What in the world is the matter with you, Fred?" I asked him. "You try your best to cause trouble."

Immediately Fred began to make excuses. Believe me, no boy in the class had more excuses or better ones — his father, his stepmother, his three-year battle with the third-grade teacher, his poor eyesight and even poorer hearing. I heard him out. Then I said, "Okay, Fred, I believe you. I know your stepmother is hard on you at home. I know Mrs. Wilbert failed you twice. But soon you'll be a man. What are you going to say if something doesn't go well at work? Are you going to say, 'It's not my fault, boss. I had a tough time when I was a kid'; or, 'I'd be a good worker if it hadn't been for my third-grade teacher'?"

To my surprise, Fred laughed. He seemed to know that even though life had not been fair to him, he would have to be responsible for his own behavior. Fred was becoming realistic about his family. He was beginning to see that no matter what his family could or could not do for him, he was going to have to grow up and take responsibility for himself — what he did and what he became.

I wish I had said to Fred, "Welcome the surprises," because what Fred did not realize at the time was that God's grace can and does surprise us. God can use even bad situations to strengthen us and help us to grow. God can break into lives that may seem closed to any new possibilities. In fact, this is what happened to Fred. A neighbor gave him a part-time job on his farm, and Fred was good at it. For the first time in his life, Fred saw himself as a person who could do well a job that was worth doing. I see that as God's grace acting in Fred's life.

Your family may have given you more than Fred's family could give him. Like Fred, though, you must begin to take responsibility for what you do and for what you will become. I hope that you, like Fred, will be able to welcome the surprises.

Who Is My Neighbor?

One day a lawyer came to Jesus with a question. "Teacher," he asked, "what shall I do to inherit eternal life?" Jesus asked his questioner what was written in the law. The man replied, "You shall love the Lord your God with all your heart, and with all your strength, and with all your mind; and your neighbor as yourself."

"You have answered right," Jesus said. "Do this and you will live."

But the lawyer was not satisfied with Jesus' reply. It was as though he was annoyed that Jesus should handle his profound question in such a simple fashion. He felt the commandment should be analyzed and defined. And so he asked, "Who is my neighbor?" Who is this person I am supposed to love as I love myself?

Jesus answered by telling the lawyer a story — the parable of the Good Samaritan.

"A man," Jesus said, "was going down from Jerusalem to

Jericho, and fell into the hands of robbers, who stripped him, beat him, and went away, leaving him half dead. Now by chance a priest was going down that road; and when he saw him, he passed by on the other side. So likewise a Levite, when he came to the place and saw him, passed by on the other side. But a Samaritan while traveling came near him; and when he saw him, he was moved with pity. He went to him and bandaged his wounds, having poured oil and wine on them. Then he put him on his own animal, brought him to an inn, and took care of him. The next day he took out two denarii [about two days wages for a laborer], gave them to the innkeeper, and said, 'Take care of him; and when I come back, I will repay you whatever more you spend.'" (Luke 10:30-35, NRSV).

At the end of the story, Jesus asked the lawyer, "Which of these three [the priest, the Levite, or the Samaritan] do you think proved himself neighbor to the man who fell among the robbers?"

As you read the story in Luke, you will notice that Jesus never answered the lawyer's original question, "What shall I do to inherit eternal life?" Neither did Jesus answer his second question, "Who is my neighbor?" The lawyer wanted Jesus to build a neat fence around God's requirements. Instead, Jesus told a story about a person in need and a man from a despised race who came to his rescue — a story that tore down all those neat fences. There are no limits to love, the story seems to say. Love of God makes us neighbors to all God's people.

The priest and the Levite had neighbors. That is, there were people for whom they felt responsible. But this half-dead man lying by the side of a lonely road — he was not their business.

He was not the business of the Samaritan traveler, either. The road was dangerous, and the bandits who had attacked the wounded man might still be there, hidden in the shadows of the rocks. Besides, this man was a Jew, and there was the same kind of mistrust and hatred between Jews and Samaritans in those days as there is between Israelis and Palestinians today. All Samaritans knew how the Jews despised them and how they in turn despised all Jews. Yet this Samaritan made himself a neighbor to his enemy. He paid the man's bills out of his own pocket and left without asking for or even expecting thanks for what he had done.

The lawyer began the conversation by asking a religious question — about eternal life. Jesus sent him away with the idea that life with God, eternal life, cannot be separated from life with other people. It sounds as though Jesus is saying, "The next person you meet is your neighbor. All people, whatever their race or condition, are your neighbors, and you are theirs. There are no limits to God's neighborhood. You cannot enjoy the life God means for you to have without caring for one another."

Modern-day Samaritan

While I was thinking about what it means to be a neighbor in today's world, I came upon a true story in Dr. Robert Coles' book entitled *The Spiritual Life of Children*. The story is one that a fifth-grader named Ginny tells. Ginny lives in a run-down neighborhood in a large city. Her father was crippled in a car accident, and her mother suffers from heart trouble and can't work outside the home. The family barely gets by, dependent as they are on disability payments and welfare.

"I was walking home the other afternoon," Ginny told me, "and there was a lady I'd never met before, not far from our house. She was old, with white hair, and I went to her and asked her what's the trouble, because she was talking to herself, I thought. She didn't hear me at first, but then she did. I asked her again, 'Can I help you?' She said, 'Oh, little girl, if you could, that would be wonderful.' I didn't like her calling me 'little girl.' I'm not a 'little girl.' I'm not even 'little' for my age. I looked at her and I was going to tell her that she isn't any bigger than I am. . . .

"[But] I calmed down and I tried to keep talking with her, and not feel huffy with her. . . . Then she told me she was trying to get to see her daughter; she's moved near here. But she'd taken a wrong turn. She showed me the directions, and I figured that out. I was going to tell her where she'd gone wrong, and I started to, but she couldn't get what I was telling her. I didn't know what to do. I had to be home; I had my chores to do. But I thought to myself: Hey, this right here is a chore you'd better do, and then you can go home. . . .

"I just made a snap decision. I told her, 'Missus, if you come with me, I'll get you to where you're going.' She wasn't sure I meant what I said! She kept clutching that piece of paper, and asking me where we were — even though I'd already told her. I decided not to argue with her. . . . I just kept walking, and I gave her a tour — I told her about the stores and the short cuts and I told her where the phones are. I asked her where she lived, and pretty soon she was telling me everything. She'd lost her husband, and her son had been in Vietnam, just like my dad and my uncle. He got killed! . . . Her [the daughter's] husband was a soldier over there, too. He came back and he had a job and everything was great, but then he got sick, and now he's in a hospital . . . and he's 'half paralyzed,' she said. She said it was terrible — that she can walk, and she's way older than he is. I didn't know what to say. I was going to say that it's like that, life, but I felt stupid telling her that; she already knew!

"We kept walking and I didn't need those directions, but she was afraid I'd get lost without them, so I pretended I was following them. I'd look at the piece of paper, and make her think I'd been saved by it! We got to be pretty good friends by the time we were there, where her daughter lives, and her grandchildren. She was tired. She was breathing heavy. I'd had to walk so slow; and I guess she'd been walking fast for her — to keep up with me. I felt bad for her. I tried to be 'considerate.' Mom says, 'Always try to be considerate.'

"Anyway, I said goodbye to her, and she said thank you so many times I thought she'd never stop! She grabbed my arm, and she said God sent me to her, and she'd pray to Him later, before she went to sleep, to thank Him for me, for having me be there. I didn't know what to say. I wasn't sure, at first, she was serious. But I looked at her, and she had tears in her eyes, so I knew she was. I was going to tell her it was an accident we'd met, but I decided not to. I just thanked her for saying such a nice thing to me. She gave me a kiss, and I left. On the way home I wondered if I'd live to be old like her, and if I'd meet some kid then, and she'd be like me. Maybe God puts you here and He gives you these hints of what's ahead, and you should pay attention to them, because that's Him speaking to you."

A Definition of Love

In Jesus' story, the Good Samaritan was a person who obeyed the commandment "You shall love the Lord your God . . . and your neighbor as yourself." The Samaritan risked his own life and fortune to save and care for the life of a stranger. For the Samaritan and for Ginny, the lives of strangers became, for a time, as valuable to them as their own.

Jesus went even further. He died for the sake of his friends and his enemies. Jesus calls us his friends and asks us to love others as he has loved us.

How can we obey such a command? Ginny was able to help the lost stranger, but suppose that old woman had been a homeless beggar? What could Ginny have done then? There are people like Mother Teresa, who left her comfortable home and went to serve the dying beggars in the streets of India. Similarly, there are people in our own country who have devoted their lives to helping the homeless. But I don't believe many of us will be able to leave home and go into the streets as these folks have.

Jesus commands us to love one another as he has loved us, but this seems impossible. How can we love as Jesus loves?

Even when we try, we soon fail and become discouraged.

A wise teacher helped me look at the commandments of Jesus in a new way. When we look at the commandments of Jesus as laws to be obeyed, he said, of course we are discouraged. "Be perfect," Jesus says, and we know we cannot be perfect. "Go and sin no more," Jesus says, and we know perfectly well that we will sin again and again. But the good news of Jesus — what we call the gospel — is not a set of impossible rules but possibility. Hear the good news, Jesus is saying. Know how much God loves you; be a part of God's kingdom, and the possibilities for your life are limitless. If you keep your eyes on rules, you will always stumble. Look up and see the wideness of God's love, and as you live more and more in the certainty of God's love for you, you will begin to discover that many things you thought impossible become possible — even loving your neighbor.

God's love for us and our love for each other is all of a piece. As we begin to open our lives to the great love God wants to give us, we will find that we can also begin to reach out to others. As Ginny's story suggests, this beginning is not likely to be a great act of heroism, but it could well be a new attitude toward others.

Some years ago a local social agency asked my husband and me if we would be temporary foster parents for two brothers who had been brought to the United States from war-torn

Cambodia. We were asked because two of our own four children are adopted, and the social agency had already okayed us as suitable parents.

I was happy to say yes to this request. Here was a real opportunity, it seemed to me, to live out Jesus' commandment. I could be a Samaritan, tending those in need. It didn't occur to me that I might have difficulty being a foster parent. In fact, I felt a bit smug. America would be a strange place for these Asian boys, but at least they would be coming to the home of a woman who knew how to cook rice properly. I hadn't lived in Asia all those years for nothing.

But the reality was different from my imagining. Oh, they liked my rice all right, and all in all the first few days went well, but then real problems began to arise. I had thought of myself as a pretty decent mother — not an A+ mom, of course, but a B- or at least a C+ mom. But all at once I felt that I was flunking as a foster mother. I had to ask myself why, and I realized that the problem was in my attitude.

When yet another crisis presented itself, I heard the voice inside my head say, "I can't really deal with that — they'll only be here a few weeks"; or "Thank goodness, they'll be gone soon." It dawned on me that I was treating two other persons as though they were disposable, rather like Kleenex. The more I thought about it, the worse I felt. Wasn't this exactly why crimes were committed, why, on a larger scale, wars were fought? Someone thought some other human being was disposable.

After the Gulf War, when American leaders were giving thanks for the loss of "so few lives," I remembered all over again my experience as a foster mother. How could we regard the lives of all those thousands who died in Kuwait and Iraq as of so little value? Were they disposable in God's sight? Surely not. We may have thought of them as our enemies or the wives and children of our enemies, but to God each one was as real and as precious as you and I.

You may have heard the story of the small boy who was taken by his mother and his much older sister to a restaurant for dinner. When the waitress came to their table, she took the orders of the mother and sister first and then turned to the child. "And what will you have, young man?"

"I'll order for him," said the mother.

The waitress acted as though she hadn't heard. "What will you have, young man?" she said again.

The sister got impatient. "I'll order for him."

"What will you have, young man?" the waitress asked again.

"A hamburger!" The little boy's eyes were shining.

"With or without onions?"

"With!"

"Toasted or plain bun?"

"Toasted!"

The waitress went to fill the orders, and the happy little boy turned to his mother. "Mother!" he said. "She thinks I'm real!"

To love someone is to know that they are real. Adults, as you well know, often fail to treat children as real persons. How often when you were small did a friend of the family or a relative insist on kissing you or pinching your cheeks without permission — without even stopping to think whether or not you might like such treatment? Then there are those who talk about you to your parents as though you don't exist or can't hear. "Do you think those teeth will ever straighten out?" "Terribly shy, isn't she?" "My, he's gotten chubby since last year."

Most of you who have moved to a new neighborhood and gone to a new school may remember a time when you were nobody. If people spoke to you, they did it in a superior since-you-don't-even-know-where-the-lunchroom-is-I-will-be-very-kind-and-show-you tone of voice. But most of the time you were ignored.

In one way or another, all of us understand the feeling of being out of it — of being treated as inferior, as invisible, as disposable, or, at any rate, as not fully deserving of respect. None of us likes to be ignored or have our feelings hurt. And an understanding of how we feel is good preparation for loving our neighbors. Because our neighbors do not like to be ignored or regarded as disposable or treated as inferior, either.

There are some things we cannot do immediately to help neighbors in need. But as we come to realize God's great love for us, we can take the first important step — we can begin today to regard each person we meet as a person with needs and feelings and ambitions and fears that are as important to him or her as ours are to us. I need to remember that God loves the homeless man begging on the street just as God loves me. God cares for him as God cares for me. Both of us are important and valuable to God.

A youth group I know of began to ask themselves what they as young people could do about hunger and homelessness. First, they had a food drive, collecting canned goods for our town's food bank, where people in need can go and get emergency food supplies. Then they offered to cook a meal in the Good Samaritan Haven, a house where people can go and get a good meal and a bed for the night. This summer they are planning to volunteer their labor when Habitat for Humanity builds another new house for a family in our community. The more they study and think about the problems of hunger and homelessness, the more possibilities for help seem to open up. I haven't heard that they've written letters to the newspaper or contacted their legislators yet, but these are other steps they might want to take. They could urge their political leaders to look at the causes for hunger and home-lessness in our community and nation and world and take steps to combat them.

God Paves the Way

When the old woman told Ginny that God had sent Ginny to help her, Ginny was surprised. "I was going to tell her it was an accident we'd met. . . ." But was it? Once during the time that I lived in Japan, I was trying to get up the courage to invite a friend of mine to go to a church service with me when she surprised me by saying, "I'd really like to go to church, but I don't know anyone to go with." I was startled, but should I have been? God loved Eiko just as God loved me. God was already at work in her heart. She didn't know God's love yet, so at that time she didn't know that God was with her. She simply felt that she might find some meaning for her life in the church. I believe God had put this hope in her heart and brought her to a person who could introduce her to the church.

As she became a part of the fellowship of the church, she came to know God's love for her and to know herself as part of the family of God. This new life made Eiko able to do something that before she might have thought was impossi-ble. She went back to school and became a social worker. And ever since she finished college, she has worked with some of the most isolated people in the world — people who, because they have the disease of leprosy, live out their lives on a tiny island off the coast of Japan, separate from the rest of society. For thirty years now, my friend Eiko has been their friend, sharing with them the love of God and the good news about Jesus that she has come to know.

Serving God

There is another parable about neighbors in Jesus' teaching. Jesus is telling a story about judgment. The king in the parable is separating the "sheep" from the "goats" — those who are to be welcomed into his kingdom from those who are to be turned away.

"Then," Jesus says, "the King will say to those at his right hand, 'Come, O blessed of my Father, inherit the kingdom prepared for you from the foundation of the world; for I was hungry and you gave me food, I was thirsty and you gave me drink, I was a stranger and you welcomed me, I was naked and you clothed me, I was sick and you visited me, I was in prison and you came to me.'"

The people to whom the king speaks are astonished. "Lord," they ask, "when did we see thee hungry and feed thee, or thirsty and give thee drink? And when did we see thee a stranger and welcome thee, or naked and clothe thee? And when did we see thee sick or in prison and visit thee?"

And the king answers, "Truly, I say to you, as you did it to one of the least of these my brethren, you did it to me."

He then turns to those on his left hand and sends them away for failing to help him when he was hungry, thirsty, a stranger, naked, sick, and in prison.

This group is equally astonished. They protest the king's harsh judgment, for if they had ever seen their Lord in such need, they insist, they would surely have helped him.

To which the king replies, "Truly, I say to you, as you did it not to one of the least of these, you did it not to me" (Matt. 25:31-46).

As we seek to make ourselves neighbors to others, then, we can know that our efforts are not wasted; rather, as the parable illustrates, they are doubly important. For we are not only serving our neighbors but also serving Jesus Christ himself. There are times when what we do will not be appreciated. There will be times when, try as hard as we can, we will make a muddle of things. Perhaps at such times this parable can be of comfort to us. Jesus does not despise our attempts to be neighbors; he accepts them as gifts to himself. On the other hand, the parable warns us that when we fail to care for those in need, we are failing to care for our Lord.

I have heard some preachers use this parable as a scare tactic. If you don't feed the hungry, welcome the stranger, or clothe the naked, God is going to damn you to hell. This is a variation on the sermon that says if you don't say exactly the right words or walk the straight and narrow path or believe exactly what I teach, watch out on the Day of Judgment. But either picture gives us a God who seems to take satisfaction in destroying people. This is not the God of Jesus Christ. In the words of a Czech pastor, "The Lord's judgment means putting things right, not destroying them." The work of Jesus is reconciliation — the restoring of right relationships between God and humankind, between neighbor and neighbor, between persons and nature, and Jesus calls us to be a part of that great enterprise. Our acts may seem quite small — like Ginny's helping the lost woman find her daughter's home, or the youth group's collecting canned goods for the community food bank. But if we fail to do the small acts of caring that are right in front of us, we probably won't be able to do the great acts that need to be done when we are confronted by them.

One woman who devoted her life to caring for neighbors in need was Dorothy Day. For many years she ran a soup kitchen and shelter for the hungry and homeless in New York City. This is her message to those who are young:

"One of the greatest evils of the day," she says, "is [a] sense of futility. Young people say what good can one person do?

What is the sense of our small effort? They cannot see that we must lay one brick at a time, take one step at a time. We can be responsible only for the one action of the present moment. But we can beg for an increase of love in our hearts that will vitalize and transform all our individual actions, and know that God will take them and multiply them, as Jesus multiplied the loaves and fishes."

What Is My Purpose?

Recently I had a long conversation with a man who told me that his father had died when he was nine years old. "That must have been very hard," I said.

"It was terrible for me," he said. "My mother was a wonderful woman, but she had no idea how to manage money or even earn it. So not only did my brother and I lose our father, but we went overnight from being normal, middle-class kids who lived in a nice neighborhood to being dirt poor. We still lived in the neighborhood, but we weren't like anyone else who lived there. We would have one pound of hamburger to last the three of us for a month. My mother didn't believe in welfare. My father had had cancer, so we were left with a lot of debts from doctors and hospital bills. Whenever there was any money, Mom always used it to pay off some of the debt. I remember the principal of my school calling me into the office one day. He told me that the school had a dress code, and I was not to wear the same pair of pants every day. He didn't know that that was the only pair of pants I owned, and I was too humiliated to tell him."

"But you turned out all right," I said. "You not only went to college, but you became a college professor. How did that happen?"

He smiled. "I was a crazy little kid," he said. "I was shattered when my father died. I couldn't understand how such a thing could happen to me. I had always loved books, and I decided that in books I could somehow find the meaning to life. That's all I wanted to know — what was the meaning of life? I read all the time. That's why I became a teacher — I'm still reading, trying to find the answer to that question. What is the meaning of life?"

The two of us talked a long time. That is, he talked and I listened. I have gone over and over that conversation in my mind. What is the meaning of life? What is the meaning of all life? What is the meaning of human life — past, present, and future? What is the meaning of my life?

Why Are We Here?

When I was eight, my Aunt Katherine decided to teach me the Westminster Shorter Catechism. The Westminster Shorter Catechism, in case you've never heard of it, was compiled by the Westminster Assembly in England and adopted for use in 1647. It's a series of 107 questions and answers about the Christian faith. It's called "Shorter" because it is shorter than the Westminster Larger Catechism.

My Aunt Katherine believed that every Presbyterian child should memorize the Shorter Catechism. I was her name-sake, so she was determined that I should recite the cate-chism at the tender age of eight and break some kind of local record. All that summer she made me follow her around the farm. She knew all the questions by heart, so while we were feeding the chickens she would call out to me, "What is God?" And I would have to answer without so much as a pause to think: "God is a Spirit, infinite, eternal, and unchangeable in his being, wisdom, power, holiness, justice, goodness, and truth."

Weeding the garden would mean a steady stream of ques-tions: "What is sin?" "What is sanctification?" "What is for-bidden in the Second Commandment?" I was supposed to deliver the answer immediately. And no peeking into the lit-tle pink book in my pocket.

Looking back, I expect Aunt Katherine did care whether or not I understood what I was saying. But at the time, what seemed to matter wasn't the meaning of those questions and answers but my ability to fire off the answer to whichever question she chose to ask.

I can't remember many of those 107 answers now, but I do

remember the first question: "What is the chief end of man?" Which, come to think of it, is the same question the college professor asked himself when his father died — What is the meaning of life? What is the chief or primary purpose of human life?

The answer I memorized for my Aunt Katherine all those years ago was this: "Man's chief end is to glorify God, and to enjoy him forever."

So what is that answer, written in the language of the seventeenth century, supposed to mean to us today?

I think it means that our chief purpose — whether man, woman, or child — is both to worship, adore, and exalt God and to enjoy God — and these two sides to our relationship with God go on forever. If we have any notion of God, we probably have some idea that we should worship or glorify God — but enjoy? "Enjoy" is a word we use in a very ordinary sense. We enjoy a good book. We enjoy playing tennis or softball. We enjoy being with our friends. Are we meant to take this same kind of pleasure in God?

The only way I can understand this is by looking at the accounts of Jesus' life. People really enjoyed his company. In fact, Jesus had such a good time that the proper religious folks were a bit scandalized. They thought a truly pious person should be more solemn, less fun-loving.

Is it possible that part of the meaning of life is for us to know this kind of pleasure in God's company? When we speak of loving God, perhaps what we mean is experiencing not only the awe that God inspires simply by being God, but also the joy of knowing God, the joy of being in God's delightful company.

My Purpose Here and Now

But can we leave it at that? Can we conclude that our purpose in life, our meaning has nothing to do with the world we live in — our families, our neighbors, our enemies?

The Bible certainly won't let us do that. Over and over again our relationship to God is tied to our relationships to one another. Jesus taught his disciples to pray "Forgive us our debts [sins], as we also have forgiven our debtors" (Matt. 6:12). And the writer of the first letter of John says, "Those who say, 'I love God,' and hate their brothers or sisters, are liars; for those who do not love a brother or sister whom they have seen, cannot love God whom they have not seen" (4:20, NRSV).

Jesus' Life and My Life

Surely the meaning of my life is tied to the meaning of Jesus' life. When he tried to tell the people in his hometown about himself, he read from the prophet Isaiah:

> "The Spirit of the Lord is upon me,
> because he has anointed me to preach good news to
> the poor.
> He has sent me to proclaim release to the captives
> and recovering of sight to the blind,
> to set at liberty those who are oppressed,
> to proclaim the acceptable year of the Lord."
>
> (Luke 4:18-19)

In another place Jesus said, "I came that they may have life, and have it abundantly" (John 10:10).

Jesus saw his life as a life lived for other people. And he saw his death as a sacrifice for others.

So when I ask myself, "What is the purpose of my life?" I have to ask this, it seems to me, in the light of Jesus' life. Is my purpose to make money? Is it to be famous? Is it to write good books? Is it to take care of my family? Is it to be a good citizen? While none of these purposes are wrong in themselves, do I want any of them to be my chief purpose — my "chief end," as the catechism says?

Do I want an answer to any of these questions to be my answer to the question "What is the meaning of life?" That is a huge question. I want my answer to be worthy. So I need to ask that question often and examine the way I am using my time — the way I am living from day to day — to see how my life is answering that question.

God has given me certain gifts. These gifts ought to give me a clue to what the meaning, the purpose of my life is. How am I using these gifts? Am I wasting my gifts? Ignoring them? Abusing them? Using them for selfish ends? Am I enjoying them? Am I trying to use them in a way that will glorify God? Am I seeking to use them to honor and bring joy to other people?

The Eternal Dimension

When people struggle to understand the meaning or the purpose of their lives, there is another question that seems to follow: Is this life all there is? Yes, some people say. This life is all we have, so live it up. Eat, drink, and be merry, for tomorrow we die! There are other people who believe that this life is all we have so we should live as responsibly as possible — make our one life count. In Buddhism and Hinduism there is the belief that we have many lives on this earth. If we live well, we will come back again in a better life, but if we are evil, we might return as a lower life form, as an animal or an insect.

From earliest times, people have wondered not only what

life means, but what death is.

What Is Death?

Have you ever thought about death? It is the one experience after birth that everyone will have. It makes sense for people to think about it and get ready for it, but instead, they seem to avoid the subject. It's hard for all of us, especially when we're young, to believe that someday we ourselves will die.

Death, for most of us, is something that happens to other people. We tend to think of it as something that doesn't touch us, and yet it's part of our daily lives. The papers are full of stories about people who have died. You can't count the number of deaths that occur on television in a week of programming. Most of us enjoy a good murder mystery. So, in one sense, we live with death every day.

But the deaths of people in print or on the screen don't usually bother us very much because they're so remote from our actual lives. Death becomes real when someone we know and care about dies. Then we begin to ask questions. We want to know what has happened to our loved one. We want to be assured that death is not the end.

The line between physical life and death is so fine that often a doctor has trouble saying at just what moment the line was crossed. But before long, the difference between the living person and the dead body becomes apparent. The body begins to deteriorate, and the person we have known is gone.

There are many causes of death — accident, disease, war, old age. Much is being done and more ought to be done to prevent disease and accidents and war. But we will never be able to prevent death — we will only be able to delay it. For death is a natural part of the kind of world in which we live.

Why Fear Death?

If death happens to us all, why are people afraid of it? Although physical death is a natural event, there is still something about the pain, the separation, and the mystery of death that makes us human beings rebel against it.

We dread the loneliness that the death of a loved one causes. When we think of our own deaths, life seems very precious. We cannot bear to think that one day it will end. Then, too, we fear the unknown. Many people, whether they are Christian or not, believe that death is not the end — that somehow a person's spirit continues to live after his or her body has died. But details of that future life are unknown, and people are afraid of what they cannot see, just as children are afraid of the dark.

The Bible suggests another reason why people fear death. "The sting of death is sin," says Paul (1 Cor. 15:56). In other words, we who know that God wants us to live as beloved children know that we often are disobedient and rebellious. We know we have failed God, and we are afraid that death will bring us directly under God's judgment. If we think of God as being like a human judge who sentences wrongdoers to punishment, this can be a very frightening picture indeed. We need to remember that God's judgment is meant to set things right, not to destroy us.

Dying to Sin

In biblical language sin and death are close relatives because it is sin that separates us from God, who is the giver of life. Sin cuts us off from God because in sin we deliberately choose to center our lives around ourselves. We turn away from God when only God's love can bring life. When we cut ourselves off from God's love, we have chosen spiritual death.

The good news of the gospel is that God in Jesus Christ has taken the consequences of human sin — death and separation from God — upon himself. "Christ died for our sins," says Paul in 1 Corinthians 15:3. And in his letter to the Romans, he explains that in baptism we are united in Christ's death — that we are "dead to sin" (6:11).

Death to sin is the first death a Christian has to face. We must let go of our self-centeredness so that Christ may live in us. Most of us cling to some of that old selfishness that ought to be dead and buried. In fact, in this life, none of us is ever fully free of sin so that God's love can fill us completely. We can only trust God for forgiveness and for the power to grow more like Christ each day. But Paul always reminds us of the good news. It is not for our goodness that God loves us. It was "while we were yet sinners" that Christ loved us and gave himself for us (Rom. 5:8).

Can you remember a time when you were small that you did something "bad" and were terrified that your mother or father would find out? What was your relationship to your parents during that time? I'd guess that it was strained and unnatural. Outwardly you tried to act as if nothing was the matter, but on the inside you were terrified that your wrong-doing would be discovered and punished.

But if you had the kind of loving parents I had, it was really a great relief when the whole business came out in the open. Your parents didn't destroy you; they did everything in their power to set things right again between you and them and between you and whomever else you may have wronged. If you stole something, they may have gone with you to the store and helped you return it to the owner. If you damaged someone's property, they may have insisted that you pay for the damage. These were "judgments," but they were positive judgments, meant to set things right. Your parents did these things because they loved you and wanted to restore a happy relationship between you and them again. Without this judgment, you would remain in fear. You would not be able to enjoy their love.

Resurrection with Christ

The Bible teaches us that physical death is not the end of life. God guarantees forgiveness and new life to us in the resurrection of Jesus from the dead. The resurrection shows God's victory over both physical and spiritual death. The Bible teaches us that we are united to Christ in his death and that we are also raised with him to new life which is eternal.

This new, eternal life begins here and now. We are "alive" when we accept God's gift of life and allow the love of Christ to fill our lives.

Some people fear that if they allow Christ to rule their lives, their own personalities will be erased. Quite the opposite is true. The closer our relationship with Christ and the more his love fills our lives, the more free we are to become the persons God has created us to be.

Resurrection of the Body

When we recite the Apostles' Creed, we say, "I believe in . . . the resurrection of the body." What do these words mean?

First of all, they do not mean that Christians are supposed to believe that a person's physical body will someday literally rise from the dead, reassembling all the elements which long before had become a part of the earth in which the body was buried. Paul answers this question in 1 Corinthians 15. He says that in the resurrection, a person will receive not his old, earthly body but a new, spiritual body. Just as our physical bodies are marvelously fitted for life on this earth, so our spiritual bodies will be fit for life beyond death.

Second — and this may sound contradictory — we don't believe that a person can be divided into two parts called "soul" (an eternal part) and "body" (a physical part). The Greek philosophers spoke in these terms, but the Hebrews and early Christians did not separate persons this way. The more we learn about the human body and the human personality, the more we see that the Hebrews were right. That which people call you is not by any means simply your physical body, but at the same time it is not some mysterious essence unrelated to your body.

Your "soul" is not something that hops into your body at birth and hops out when you die, although there are people who have this idea. In medieval times there were even "scientists" who wanted to prove or disprove the existence of the soul, and so they weighed bodies immediately before and after death to see if the body was lighter, thinking that a "weight loss" would indicate that something had left. This makes about as much sense as the declaration of an early astronaut who said that since he had been to outer space and had not seen God, that proved that there was no such being.

I realize I'm tramping about in territory that no one can be sure about, but it seems to me that when the Bible or the creed speaks of the resurrection of the body, it means by "body" the whole personality, the whole self. It means that you, the self that you are and know — this is the self that dies with Christ and is resurrected with Christ. This is the person who is a citizen of the kingdom of heaven. Our physical bodies will not be resurrected as they are, for, as Paul says, they would not be appropriate for life in our new environment. But we will be recognizably those same selves we have been talking about all along.

Completing the Incomplete

There have been hints throughout this book that there is something incomplete about this world and those of us who live in it. There is much in nature and in human nature that remains to be "tamed" — to be set right. There is much that is not yet in harmony with God's purpose for creation. If we compare God's work in the world to the acts in a drama, we can say that the play isn't over yet. Sin and death still exist, but with Christ's victory over sin and death, we know that the last act of the drama has begun. We can look forward with confidence to the end of the play, when God's work of reconciliation, of setting right, will be completed, and the kingdom of this world shall become "the kingdom of our Lord and of his Christ" (Rev. 11:15).

The end of the drama will contain the judgment and the remaking of the world. To say that judgment means to set right does not mean that what people do doesn't matter. God loves us, and that means that God pays us the compliment of taking our actions seriously.

In God's judgment, evil will be fully exposed: both the polite sins like pride, hypocrisy, jealousy, and selfishness, which can sometimes be hidden from other people, and those sins that are more difficult to conceal, such as murder, adultery, and theft. God sees through our every pretension; God sees us more clearly than we can ever see ourselves. But God's will is not to destroy but to set all things right.

Recently I was cutting a watermelon and because of my careless use of a very sharp knife found myself in the emergency room. The nurse in charge washed the cut in my hand very carefully and put a powerful antiseptic on it. Then the doctor poked me with a hypodermic needle and began to sew up my hand. It was not a happy experience, and yet, if the nurse and the doctor had not taken my cut seriously or had merely lectured me on my carelessness, I might not have been able to type the manuscript of this book.

In much the same way, God's judgment is a gift of healing, a gift of love. If we refuse to accept it, we will find ourselves refusing God's love. But God is not a bully — that love will not be forced down our throats if we are unwilling to receive it.

The Bible also joins words of judgment with the promise of re-creation. Judgment clears the way for the creation of a new heaven and a new earth. The Bible paints this new creation in vivid, awe-inspiring, sometimes puzzling word pictures, as though to stretch our imaginations as far as possible, for mere words cannot describe the final plans God has for us.

Since all our views of the new creation are expressed in picture language, I would like to add another picture. This one is taken from fiction. You may have already read it. It comes from C. S. Lewis's *The Last Battle*.

The excerpts I've chosen come from the last of seven books that tell the stories of several children from our world who go through a magic wardrobe and find themselves involved in the history of another world. The country of Narnia, of which some of the children are made kings and queens, is populated with talking animals and mythical creatures. The true King of Narnia is the wise and powerful Lion, Aslan, son of the Emperor-over-sea. After a great battle between the followers of the noble Aslan and the forces of evil, Aslan's followers leave Narnia and enter a new land through the door of a stable. Narnia is plunged into darkness, but the land they enter reminds them of the beautiful country that they left behind:

> It was the Unicorn who summed up what everyone was feeling. He stamped his right forehoof on the ground and neighed and then cried:
>
> "I have come home at last! This is my real country! I belong here. This is the land I have been looking for all my life, though I never knew it till now. The reason why we loved the old Narnia is that it sometimes looked a little like this. . . . Come further up, come further in!" . . .
>
> Everyone you had ever heard of (if you knew the history of those countries) seemed to be there. . . . And there was greeting and kissing and handshaking and old jokes revived (you've no idea how good an old joke sounds when you take it out again after a rest of five or six hundred years) and the whole company moved forward. . . .

The light ahead was growing stronger. Lucy saw that a great series of many-coloured cliffs led up in front of them like a giant's staircase. And then she forgot everything else, because Aslan himself was coming, leaping down from cliff to cliff like a living cataract of power and beauty.

. . . Then Aslan turned to them and said:

"You do not yet look so happy as I mean you to be."

Lucy said, "We're so afraid of being sent away, Aslan. And you have sent us back into our own world so often."

"No fear of that," said Aslan. "Have you not guessed?"

Their hearts leaped and a wild hope rose within them.

"There was a real railway accident," said Aslan softly. "Your father and mother and all of you are — as you used to call it in the Shadow-Lands — dead. The term is over: the holidays have begun. The dream is ended: this is the morning."

And as He spoke He no longer looked to them like a lion; but the things that began to happen after that were so great and beautiful that I cannot write them. And for us this is the end of all the stories, and we can most truly say that they all lived happily ever after. But for them it was only the beginning of the real story. All their life in this world and all their adventures in Narnia had only been the cover and the title page: now at last they were beginning Chapter One of the Great Story, which no one on earth has read: which goes on for ever: in which every chapter is better than the one before.

Our true natures can be seen only in the completed purpose of God for all creation. In this life, as wonderful as it is, we cannot know God fully, nor can we experience all God intends for us to be and to become. Death, then, is not the end of life for God's children but the beginning of "Chapter One of the Great Story."

For those of us on this side of the gate, death may seem to be an end to life and a time of sorrow and separation, but, as *The Last Battle* illustrates, those who pass through the gate can see death for what it really is — the entrance into the full experience of life with God. They greet loved ones for whom they had mourned. They find themselves in the company of the prophets and the apostles. They meet persons from all ages and nations. And when the Lord Christ welcomes them, they realize that they have come home at last.

You and I cannot really picture this scene. So this book must be left incomplete, just as our lives are incomplete until, with all of nature and all of God's children, we glorify and enjoy God in the New Creation. Only then will each of us find the full answer to the question "Who am I?"